RUNAWAYS
ROCK ZOMBIES

RUNAWAYS

ROCK ZOMBIES

WRITER: **TERRY MOORE**
PENCILER: **TAKESHI MIYAZAWA**
INKERS: **TAKESHI MIYAZAWA, NORMAN LEE** & **CRAIG YEUNG**
COVER ART: **HUMBERTO RAMOS** & **CHRISTINA STRAIN**

"MOLLIFEST DESTINY"
WRITER: **CHRIS YOST**
ARTIST: **SARA PICHELLI**

"TRUTH OR DARE"
WRITER: **JAMES ASMUS**
ARTIST: **EMMA RIOS**
COVER ART: **DAVID LAFUENTE** & **CHRISTINA STRAIN**

COLORIST: **CHRISTINA STRAIN**
LETTERER: **VC'S JOE CARAMAGNA**
EDITORS: **NICK LOWE** & **DANIEL KETCHUM**

RUNAWAYS CREATED BY **BRIAN K. VAUGHAN** & **ADRIAN ALPHONA**

COLLECTION EDITOR: **JENNIFER GRÜNWALD**
ASSISTANT EDITOR: **ALEX STARBUCK**
ASSOCIATE EDITOR: **JOHN DENNING**
EDITOR, SPECIAL PROJECTS: **MARK D. BEAZLEY**
SENIOR EDITOR, SPECIAL PROJECTS: **JEFF YOUNGQUIST**
SENIOR VICE PRESIDENT OF SALES: **DAVID GABRIEL**

EDITOR IN CHIEF: **JOE QUESADA**
PUBLISHER: **DAN BUCKLEY**
EXECUTIVE PRODUCER: **ALAN FINE**

PREVIOUSLY

AT SOME POINT IN THEIR LIVES, ALL KIDS THINK THAT THEIR PARENTS ARE EVIL. FOR MOLLY HAYES AND HER FRIENDS, THIS IS ESPECIALLY TRUE. ONE NIGHT, MOLLY AND HER FRIENDS DISCOVERED THAT THEIR PARENTS WERE A GROUP OF SUPER-POWERED CRIME BOSSES WHO CALLED THEMSELVES "THE PRIDE." USING TECHNOLOGY AND RESOURCES STOLEN FROM THEIR PARENTS, THE TEENAGERS WERE ABLE TO STOP THE PRIDE AND BREAK THEIR CRIMINAL HOLD ON LOS ANGELES. BUT THEY'VE BEEN ON THE RUN EVER SINCE.

ATTACKED BY A CREW OF MAJESDANIAN SOLDIERS INTENT ON CAPTURING THE RUNAWAYS' KAROLINA DEAN—WHOM THEY HOLD RESPONSIBLE FOR THE DESTRUCTION OF THEIR HOME PLANET—THE RUNAWAYS FIGHT BACK AND DO EVERYTHING THEY CAN TO ESCAPE. BUT WHEN THEY REALIZE THAT THIS IS A FIGHT THEY WON'T BE ABLE TO WIN, THE SHAPESHIFTING XAVIN TAKES KAROLINA'S PLACE AND WILLINGLY AGREES TO GO WITH THE MAJESDANIANS, LEAVING HER FELLOW RUNAWAYS BEHIND.

7

Whoa! No fair, Victor jumped the start.
No I didn't. You guys are slow.
Hellooo, we're not guys.
Helloo, check the screen.

Out of the way, fat boy!
Molly! You pushed me off the...
Ha Ha! I'm winning!
You're next, Klara.
Not if you can't catch me.

No fair, Victor! You went off course, you're out!
I'm in, Princess, and you've got payback written all over your...
Klara, I see what you're doing with that plant.
Ha ha!
I can't see!
Klara! That is so not fair!
I know! Thank you for teaching me how to cheat.
Okay, ladies, this ends now!
Nooo! Klara, save me from this dork who talks like a bad comic book!
Save yourself! I must cheat!

Man, and I thought I was noisy. Sounds like Godzilla attacking a kindergarten down here.
Why won't you dieeee?!
Never!
Oh, good morning, Chase. How are you? I'm fine, thanks. Where are you going? Have to go to work, kids, put food on the table and game controllers in your hands. Oh, thank you, Chase. Thank you from the bottom of our wee little hearts.
AAIIEEGH!
Ha ha!
ACE DONU
Don't wait up. I may stop off at the club and have a drink with the boys. Bye, Chase! Hurry back.
I win! I win! I love cheating!
Protest! I wanna see the instant replay!
You guys play too rough!
Every once in a while, it will hit me.
What?
This. All This. Everything.

What do you mean?
I mean, it wasn't that long ago we were just kids, y'know? Living with our parents, eating their food, driving their cars...
You got to drive the car?
Not with their permission. I snuck it out once, though. Drove to Taco Bell and back. Afterwards I thought: That's it, I've left an ecological footprint. I felt so dirty.
Karolina, look, the only footprints you're leaving on this planet are in the sand.
You're sweet.
It's so great to see you smile again.
I thought the pain would never go away...but it does. It gets better.
Xavin would be proud of you.
I hope so.

There goes Chase, off to work. What a surprise, huh?
Talk about an eco footprint... that crazy Stein bus he's driving now...
I know, I can't believe he's sticking with it.
WREEEGH...
CHING-GA!
CLANG!
VROOOOM!
Chase, you freakin' ape! Way to stay under the radar, genius!
sigh

I'm not talking about old school voodoo or Romero zombies...they're too slow. I'm talking new, improved zombies. You know, Robert Rodriguez stuff.
That's Hollywood, Val. I'm afraid real life is not so attractive.
But it can be done, right? I mean, on a mass scale... you could make that happen?
All things are possible through magic, my friend. Robert Minoru said that.
Ah, I miss the Minorus. The L.A. magic scene has not been the same without them.
Good times.

Mother?
Oh, sorry. Yes, to answer your question. A simple spell attacking one's weakness is all it takes. But this is customized to the individual. To build an army of zombies by casting a spell affecting many people...I don't know.
What is the common weakness?
Debt?
No, this is a physical spell, the flaw has to be physical. Something thousands of people in L.A. have in common.
KNOCK! KNOCK!
TAP! TAP! TAP!
Yeah?
Sorry to bother you, Val. I just need you to sign some head shots when you get a chance. You know me, always promoting.
When you get a chance.
Yeah, I'll get right on it.

Val...
Mmmm?
How many people in Los Angeles would you say have had plastic surgery?
I dunno. Probably half, maybe more. Why?

CAPITOL RECORDS
Hey! *The Retching Pigs* are hurtin', man! We had a legal contract. Three records and a tour. Then this weasel sends an email tellin' us we've been dumped...!
I was just doing my job!
They dumped us by email, man! Cold!
Lay down your weapons! Nobody has to get hurt.
S.W.A.T.

Is that true, you fired them?
They're a lousy band! We leaked their record onto YouTube and it got three hits.
So you don't want to negotiate.
We don't negotiate with losers. Shoot 'em, maybe it'll boost sales.
Okay, SWAT One... proceed to Stage Two. Stage Two.
LOSERS!
Hey, hey! Tell those wall rats to back off or we start shooting!
No! Don't shoot! I'm diabetic!
RATATATATATTATAT!
I mean it...back off!

Vinnie... time for a respect check!
Hang on to your spleens!
BWAAAAUUUUUUUUUGH!
A sound garden.

What the...?! What key is that?
I don't know!
If you guys are taking requests, I have a suggestion...
Respect.
Ever heard of it? No?
I'll teach you.
Oh look, a goth hood ornament. Hey, emo...goth is dead.

Call me "emo" again, scumpuppy, and the coroner will find your mouth in a place so wrong--
You're wasting your breath on this one, Nico.
He only hears what he wants to hear.
Maybe that's why his music sucks.
Okay, now you sound like my girlfriend.
Watch, he'll say something bad and start shooting again.
And I hate my girlfriend!
RATATATATATATTATATATTATTAT!
Duck!
Told ya.
He reminds me of my husband!
Double-gross.

PLINK!
PLINK! PLINK!
Finished?
Our turn.
YAAAGH!
BPPHITTT!
BAM!
Thanks!
RA-AAKK!

SWAT One, what the hell is goin' on up there?!
You wouldn't believe me if I told you, captain. Uh...threat neutralized.
Oh great, I barely get the frog parked and you guys are already finished.
Well, not exactly fighting the cream of the crop here, are we?
Okay, we need to get out of here before somebody starts asking questions...like who's going to pay for this mess.
Oh. Right.
There. Just because they're prisoners doesn't mean they can't look pretty.
You missed a spot.
Molly, Klara...let's go.
You! Hit the deck!
We kind of already did that. Bye!

What are you doing? You don't know how to fly the frog!
Swap seats before you get us killed.
We had to go! I know how to hit the go button thingy.
Wooah... what a mess!
So, what do you think?
Good execution, nice teamwork. In and out. I think we're ready to get back to the big time. There's just one problem.
What?
Chase.
Mail call.
Thank you, Chase. Just leave it there.

So, Lydia, Lydia...they wrote a song about you, y'know.
Yeah, yeah, old Marx Brothers song, I know. Very funny.
Marks...? Eh, I was thinking of Nevermore. Metal band out of Seattle? You'd dig 'em.
Is there a reason we're talking about what bands you like while I have work to do?
Just being friendly.
Out of your league, surfer boy. When you get rich enough to buy this station, I'll be friendly.
It's just a matter of time, Lydia. Just a matter of time.
Okay now, remember, she doesn't have to listen to all of it, just through one chorus.
Right, yeah, I got it. She listens to the song and doesn't hear the spell we mixed under the chorus.
Brilliant... if it works.

Lydia, I hold in my hand the next big hit, and nobody has it but KZIT and yours truly!
Way to go, Val! Who is it?
Just a little electronic dance rap I knocked out on Garage Band...with a little something extra added in. See what you think.
Nice beat.
Turn it up.
I like it. Great dance beat.
Then let's dance! C'mon.
What do you think?
I like it! What's that chanting in the background?
What?

I said I hear chanting. What is it?
That's the surprise...
What in the world...?
Val... something's wrong. Val...
Whoa.
AAEEEIIIGHARGH!!
Lydia?

How do you feel?
WAAAUUUGH.
Is it working?
It did something. I don't know what.
Lydia, stand up!
AOOUUGH.
OOOUGHHHHH.
Holy Romero...
I'd say the test was positive, wouldn't you?
She's the most disgusting thing I've ever seen!

Well, there you have it... Lydia, the mother of our zombie army.
I love it! Today Lydia, tomorrow Los Angeles!

8
RAMOS 08

ROCKIN', ROCKIN' ALL NIGHT LONG... ROCKIN' ROCKIN' PLAYIN' OUR SONG...
Ice... need more ice... somebody...
Hey, you shot me.
Oops. Sorry.
Did anybody bring mustard? Or buns?
SLUURP!
EMBRACE
Okay, people, when I said let's go camping and do some team bonding, this is *NOT* what I had in mind!

I don't know...Klara's bonding me to death over here.
And I haven't even cheated yet.
Ice!
You shot me again.
Sorry.
We need to gather firewood for a fire.
We don't need firewood. We have footstigon.
I'm not cooking on that thing. The bus has a microwave.
Okay, now you're just doing it on purpose. Look, I'm...stop shooting me!
Sorry. Sorry. Sorry. Sorry. Sorry.
CLICK! CLICK! CLICK! CLICK! CLICK!

Everybody listen up! This is a *camp-out!* Turn off all electronic devices **EEE-MEEDIATELY!**
Chase, put that footstigon in the bus.
Klara, stop shooting Victor!
Victor, turn off that laptop!
Nico, close that book!
Karolina... put some clothes on!
Fine. Sun's going down anyway.
Since when did we start letting the kid boss us around?
She's got a point. Here we are. We might as well make the most of it.

When we get
our fire built, I
have a surprise
for you guys...
Costume designs!
Molly...
Groan!
So where are we supposed to find firewood in the desert?
Really? We're getting costumes?
Can we have petticoats?
Wow!
You get a cape made of rose petals.

...and we ended with *Japanimation Eyes* by *The Fuglees*...for those of you taking notes. You can find a list of everything we play here on KZIT at our website, broadcasting live because nobody broadcasts dead, ya freakin' bozo.
And now Uncle Val has a surprise for all his little Val-Pals out there.
A ***new*** song...
SLLLP
...guaranteed to change your life and cure what ails ya.
This song's so hot, it's the last song you'll ever need. This song's so hot, I'm gonna play it nonstop from here to eternity. This song's so hot...
It'll make you do ***baaaaad*** things! Lap it up, rock zombies.
KERR
CLICK!
BOOM! BA-DA BOOM SCREEE..

I'm not wearing anything made of spandex.
It's not spandex! It's *bodyskin...*like the swimmers wear.
Sounds good to me. I think Nico would look good in a Speedo.
Chase, you're such a perv.
I don't know, Molly. It's so... tight. I'm not used to clothes like that.
Okay, okay, the *X-Men* seem to think it works, but if you guys don't want to learn from the greatest team ever, I have some other ideas...
Here's a classic look, lots of pockets for carrying notes and secret weapons.
I was wondering what to do with all my crime-fighting notes.
Stuff 'em in your pocket protector.
Is that a boy or a girl?
Molly, sweetie... they're all very nice, but...
Okay, if you guys can't even decide on a costume, I'm not going to sing our new *theme song!*

What is that song on the radio?
I don't know. I've never heard it before.
Turn it up.
Great beat!
What?
I said...
BOOM! BA-DA BOOM SCREEE...! BOOM! BA-DA BOOM SCREEE...! BOOM! BA-DA BOOM SCRE
GREAT BEAT!
AAAAAAGH!
BOOM! BA-DA BOOM SCREEE...! BOOM! BA-DA BOOM SCREEE...! BOOM! BA-DA BOOM SCRE
EEIIIIGH!
SCREEEECH!
BOOM! BA-DA BOOM SCREEE...! BOOM! BA-DA BOOM SCREEE...! BOOM! BA-DA BOOM SCRE

CRAAASH!
!BA-DA BOOM SCREEE...! BOOM! BA-DA BOOM SCREEE...! BOOM! BA-DA BOOM SCREEE...!
EEIIIIGH!
Hey, buddy...you all right?
AAAAAAGH!
EEIIIIGH!
BA-DA BOOM SCREEE...! BOOM! BA-DA BOOM SCREEE...! BOOM! BA-DA BOOM SCREEE...!

Mornin'.
Hey, K.

Aren't you cold?
A little. You cold?
Yeah. It's, like, 30 or 20 degrees out here.
Here.
Brrrr.
Hang on...
Better?
Much.
I wish Xavin was here.
Me too, Mol.
Me too.

Okay, Val...very funny. We've all had a good laugh. Now unlock the door.
At least play a different song, dude! You're killin' us out here!
ON AIR
This is *my* time slot, Rhymin! Not cool, man. Not cool!
BOOM! BA-DA BOOM SCREEE...! BOOM! BA-DA BOOM SCREEE...! BOOM! BA-DA BOOM SCRE
So how are all my little Val-Pals doing out there in Candyland, eh? Diggin' the beat? Soak it up, ya meat puppets. Groove on Val's rhythm and release your inner zombie.
He's really lost it this time. Totally gone.
He's just playing that same stupid song over and over.
I called the police, but they said everybody's busy. Some sort of crisis in the city. We're going to have to take care of this ourselves.
AAUURRGHHHH!
AAAGH!
AUUUUGHHHH?
Looks like they don't appreciate your inner beauty, Lydia. What can I say? That's L.A. For you.

Everybody loaded up? Chase, did you put water on the fire?
No, but I spit on it for twenty minutes. How's that?
Lovely.
Hey, Molly! Klara! Time to go.
I need carbs, people. Where's the nearest IHOP?
IHOP on your own time. I need a shower.
I second that. Take me back to the house.
Let's go! Let's go! The Magic Bus doesn't like to be kept waiting!
Magic Bus?
Yeah. That's what I named my new baby. Fits, doesn't it?
Do we really need to name a car?
It's not a car, it's the Magic Bus.
Are we there yet?

BOOM! BA-DA BOOM SCREEE...! BOOM! BA-DA BOOM SCREEE...! BOOM! BA-DA BOOM SCRE
Wake up, L..A. If you can hear my voice--if you can hear this song--then you've either joined the ranks of the undead, or you know someone who has. I myself have been victimized by this cruel turn of events.
KZIT's very own promotional director and dear friend, Lydia Stumpmeyer, has fallen victim to the curious plag that is sweeping the city
BOOM! BA-DA BOOM SCREEE...! BOOM! BA-DA BOOM SCREEE....! BOOM! BA-DA BOOM SCRE
Say hi, Lydia.
Sad.
But there is hope, my friends. There is hope. And hope's name is yours truly...Val Rhymin.
Uncle Val has the cure for what ails you beautiful zombies. And I'll be more than happy to share my miracle cure for anybody who does me one little favor...

BURN THIS CITY DOWN!
BURN IT TO THE GROUND, THEN BURN THE GROUND! CAUTERIZE THIS DECREPIT TOWN AND FLUSH OUT ALL THE HYPOCRITICAL RATS THAT INFEST THE CITY OF ANGELS LIKE A CANCER.
AND WHEN YOU'VE FLUSHED OUT THE RATS, MARCH THEM INTO THE SEA! I'M TALKIN' BANKERS, POLITICIANS, MOVIE PRODUCERS AND THOSE INSIPID LITTLE DOGS IN GUCCI SWEATERS! TO THE SEA, ALL OF THEM!
Oh, and while you're at it...
TAKE THEIR MONEY!
!BA-DA BOOM SCREEE...! BOOM! BA-DA BOOM SCREEE...! BOOM! BA-DA BOOM SCREEE...!
DON'T BURN THE MONEY BECAUSE IT BELONGS TO UNCLE VAL! SAVE THE MONEY! SAVE THE JEWELS! SAVE ALL THE GOLD AND SILVER YOU CAN FIND!
WAIT, FORGET THE SILVER. SILVER'S OVERRATED. JUST BRING GOLD! MONEY, JEWELS AND GOLD!
AND A FERRARI! I WANT A FERRARI!
MONEY! JEWELS! GOLD! AND A FERRARI!
DO WHAT I TELL YOU AND MEET ME AT THE HOLLYWOOD BOWL TONIGHT AT MIDNIGHT! BRING ME THE LOOT, AND I'LL GIVE YOU THE CURE!
NOW GO, MY LITTLE MONKEYS! GOOOOOOOOO!

Is it just me or is that guy whacked?
...I'LL GIVE YOU THE CURE! NOW GO!
Val's out there, dude. He works the cutting edge of the airwaves. That's why he's a genius.
He's a nut.
BOOM! BA-DA BOOM SCREEE...! BOOM! BA-DA BOOM SCREEE...! BOOM! BA-DA BOOM SCRE
And I'm pretty sure what he's saying is illegal to say on the radio. What's the deal with all the cars...
Parked on the side of the...
1204
BOOM! BA-DA BOOM SCREEE...! BOOM! BA-DA BOOM SCREEE...! BOOM! BA-DA BOOM SCRE
Oh my stars, *turn it up!*
Now you're gettin' it.
Are you blind? ***Look!***

What? It's a radio!
At the *cars,* you idiot. Look at the *cars!*
Look at the *city.*
!BA-DA BOOM SCREEE...! BOOM! BA-DA BOOM SCREEE...! BOOM! BA-DA BOOM SCREEE...
Whoa!
It's a war zone!
That's what I'm trying to tell you!
What's goin' on?
I don't know, but it may have something to do with your BFF on the radio. Listen.
IF YOU WANT THE CURE, YOU HAVE TO BRING ME THE MONEY. HOW CAN YOU HAVE THE CURE IF YOU DON'T BRING ME THE MONEY?
You know, not everyone appreciates Val's brand of humor...
Are you kidding me? Pull off! **NOW!**
!BA-DA BOOM SCREEE...! BOOM! BA-DA BOOM SCREEE...! BOOM! BA-DA BOOM SCREEE...

SCREEEECH!!
BOOM! BA-DA BOOM SCREEE...! BOOM! BA-DA BOOM SCREEE...! BOOM! BA-DA BOOM SCRE
I hear something in this song. That chant under the music. Sounds like...
What's goin' on?
We've got trouble.
Are we out of gas?
Where am I going?
BOOM! BA-DA BOOM SCREEE...! BOOM! BA-DA BOOM SCREEE...! BOOM! BA-DA BOOM SCRE
KZIT. We're going straight to the source of this crap.
Uh, don't look now, but that may be easier said than done.
BOOM! BA-DA BOOM SCREEE...! BOOM! BA-DA BOOM SCREEE...! BOOM! BA-DA BOOM SCRE
ZOMBIES!
Eww, gross!

Oh, this is going to be so fun.
I'm with you, buddy.
What do you think you're doing?
What else do you do in a zombie RPG? Start blowin' away zombies. 10 points each, baby.
Chase, wait!
!BA-DA BOOM SCREEE...! BOOM! BA-DA BOOM SCREEE...! BOOM! BA-DA BOOM SCREEE...
These zombies aren't dead. Look. They're real people. They're just...
Really, really, really ugly.
It's the song. The chant I hear in the music must be a spell. These people are enchanted!
We can't kill them.
We have to do something. They're going to crush us in here!
AAIEGH!

Okay, seriously, we have to get out of here. And fast.
Chase, can you get this thing up in the air again?
Not without firing up the jets. You want a zombie barbeque, that's Plan A.
They're not *zombies.*
WHATEVER!
Okay, everybody just calm down and *think!* And turn off that stupid radio!
OOM! BA-DA BOOM SCREEE...! BOOM! BA-DA BOOM SCREEE...! BOOM! BA-DA BOOM SCRE
I have an idea. Chase, open the sunroof.
What do you...?
Just DO IT!
AAAUUWGHHHHH!
Let's throw a little light on the problem. Harmless, but effective.
It's working. They're backing off!
I don't know how long this will hold them. Everybody out. Hurry!

ay. Now what?
Nico, you said you heard a spell in the song. If magic turned these people into zombies, can you reverse it?
I don't think so. I can't even reverse my own spells.
It's easy. Just get out your stick and say Unzombie!
We better do something, because if they get any closer all bets are off on that peace and love crap.
Nico...? You want me to get us out of here my way?
Karolina, get the girls out of harm's way.
Check.
Hey...!
Nicooo... no more Mr. Nice Guy!
Sorry, guys, time to act!
When Blood Is Shed, Let The Staff Of One Emerge!

Zombie Not!
Uh...Nico... is this what you were tryin' to do?
Not even close.
That's... disgusting.

Don't hurt them, you said. They're just people, you said.
Nico, hit "undo!"
I told you I can't reverse spells!
Can you reverse time? Because I'd really like a do-over on this.
It's coming at us!
Okay, Molly, bad dream. Wake up. Wake up!

9

UGHWWWAUUGHH!
CRASH!
SQUASH COLA
What the heck is that thing?!
I don't know. I was just trying to reverse the zombie spell.
You said *Zombie Knot*. There's a knot of zombies.
ZOMBIE NOT! N-O-T!
Don't tell me, tell ***them!***

Molly, Klara... watch out! If this monster starts throwing things, stay under cover.
I'm not a child, Karolina, I'm a *super hero!*
There aren't any plants here! We've got to get back to the bus!
Okay, remember, those are living people on that thing. No mortal strikes!
Okay. But it's going t take a heav hand to brin it down.
Or a heavy foot.
KRRAAASH!
COLA
SCHOARRCH!
SCHOARRCH!

What was THAT?!
I'm still working on my aim! Gimme a break!
et me you how s done, lseye.
SNAP!
KRAACK!
BOOM!
Whoa! A little *warning* next time!
POP!
POW!
KRACK!
POW!
Wow! Awesome job, Super-Fart! Can I have your autograph?
Yeah, and you know where you can put it.

Let's see if a little juice will split them up.
SHOOARGHSH! SHOOARGHSH!
FAUGHOOOOW!
AUWOOOOGHOOOOOOOO!
Eww, that's **GROSS!!**
My rose! Gotta get my rose!
Oily!

SPLOOOOOOOOOSH!
Augh! Headache!
Run!
Ughf!
Look out!
Too...much... magic!
Sorry!

Aigh!
Gotcha!
Molly...thank goodness!
Yay me!
Victor, grab Nico!
Nico!
Well... puff puff... the good news is, no more creature.
And no dead people.
The bad news... spit!.. all this oil...and no masseuse.
Bet you wish you had uniforms *now*, don't ya? A that oil would ru right off a good super hero uniform. Now we gotta do laundry.
Yeah, that's what I'm worried about... laundry.

I'm sorry, guys. I don't know what's going on with my magic. The scatter spell, that creature... the oil. Everything I try is like way too much.
Maybe you're getting stronger. Do you feel stronger?
I'm not sure what I feel. I think...I don't know. Ever since my great-grandmother tortured me...
She *tortured* you?! Your own great-grand-mother?!
I told you that. She was trying to make me stronger. You were just too distracted by Lily to notice anything else.
Oof!
et's don't go er that again. I member. It just ounded odd to ear you say it like that.
That's what it is, Nico. Your great-grandmother did something to you. To your powers.
I'm okay... if anybody cares.
So, before we were so rudely interrupted...
To the radio station.
Yes.
The one in the *mall?* We're going to the *mall?!* *Yay!*

Wow, it's weird, the place being deserted like this.
This is such a rip. None of the stores are open...the food court's closed...
We're not here to shop, Molly.
Looks like the lights are off at KZIT, too.
Not to worry. I have a key.
What the...?
They're chained shut.
From the inside.
That means Val is inside, broadcasting.
Not for long.
CRAAACK!
POP!!
CRASH!
Door's open.
Not how I would have done it, but...
Remind me never to arm wrestle you.
CRUNCH!
CRUNCH!

BA-DA BOOM SCREEE...! BOOM! BA-DA BOOM SCREEE...! BOOM! BA-DA BOOM SCREEE...!
Is that where they make the shows?
Yeah, the broadcast booth.
Val calls it the Pit.
I'm sensing something here.
BA-DA BOOM SCREEE...! BOOM! BA-DA BOOM SCREEE...! BOOM! BA-DA BOOM SCREEE...!
Val? Hey, Val!
What?
I don't know. It's not unfamiliar but I can't put my finger on it.
Whoaaa.
Can you stop that stupid song from playing?
My pleasure.
BA-DA BOOM SCREEE...! BOOM! BA-DA BOOM SCREEE...! BOOM! BA-DA BOOM SCREEE...!
DROOOOOO...
CLICK!
CLICK!
CLICK!
Still playing.
Then it's not coming from here.

Help! Help, somebody!
Chase!
Chase? Where are you?
In here. Val's office!
Oh my gosh!
Lydia? Lydia...talk to me, okay? Tell me what's goin' on.
AUGHHHWWWU!
I know her. She works here. She's hot. Or she was. Don't let her jump!
MOOOAWW.
Lydia? Lydia, can you hear me?
We're here to help you.
AGHGUU?

Take my hand. Please. Come on...
Aaargh!
NO!
EEEEIGH!
Good one, Karolina.
I can get her back up here. You pull her in.
Poor thing. I feel so bad for her.
We've got to get to the bottom of this. If Lydia's any indication, people all over the city are going out of their minds. We have to find that DJ.
He must be broadcasting from the mobile truck. He could be anywhere.
Yeah. But we know where he'll be at midnight.

WAUNGGG, BOM! WHEEGH! BOOM! WAUNGGG, BOM! WHEEGH! BOOM! WAUNGGG, B
WUAAGH! WAUGH! UGH! UGH! EUEECHH!
WAUNGGG, BOM! WHEEGH! BOOM! WAUNGGG, BOM! WHEEGH! BOOM! WAUNGGG, BO
AUUUGH! AUUUGH!
We are zombies. We may pass.
WAUNGGG, BOM! WHEEGH! BOOM! WAUNGGG, BOM! WHEEGH! BOOM! WAUNGGG, B
What are you doing? Stop it!
You love me, zombie woman. You want to bake brownies for me.
That'll be the day. Shut up, will ya? I'm tryin to hear what Nico's saying.

I said, where are you, Karolina? Report.
Sorry, Chase was distracting me. We just walked in.
Don't make any sudden moves, but get to your positions quickly. It's almost midnight.
NGGG, BOM! WHEEGH! BOOM! WAUNGGG, BOM! WHEEGH! BOOM! WAUNGGG, BOM!
Hey, you guys are supposed to say Roger and Over when you talk. Over.
I told you we're not doing that, Molly. We're not the army.
I bet the Avengers say Over. Over.
I heard that.
This band is awful!
NGGG, BOM! WHEEGH! BOOM! WAUNGGG, BOM! WHEEGH! BOOM! WAUNGGG, BOM!
WUAAGH! WAUGH! UGH! UGH! EUEECHH!

BOOM! BA-DA BOOM SCREEE...! BOOM! BA-DA BOOM SCREEE...! BOOM! BA-DA BOOM SCRE
BONGGGGGG!
LAAIIEE AU ENLLMEUUGH... BAAULL RRYYEEENN!
AAUUGHOOOGHH! AAUUGHOOOGHH! AAUUGHOOOGH
Good evening! So nice of you to come! Thank you! Thank you!
Let's take him now!
No! Wait! Hear what he has to say first.

So, how was your day? Did you have *fun*? Did you bring Uncle Val lots of *presents*?
This guy is *sick!*
Patience, Karolina. The police are watching. Let him dig his own grave.
UUGHOOOOGHH! AAUUGHOOOOGHH! AAUUGHOOOOGHH!
So, I was talking to my partner the other day, and I asked him...how can we turn the Val-Pal Nation of loyal radio zombies into *real* zombies that will make me rich?
And you know what he said? He said, *"How many people in L.A. have had plastic surgery?"*
Well that's an interesting reply, don't you think? And, of course, the answer is...
EVERYBODY!
Everybody here has gone under the knife to snip, tuck, cut, puff and pluck their body into something it was never meant to be. All it took was a little *music magic* to bring the scars to the surface and...
WA-LA! ROCK ZOMBIEEEEEES!

I've heard enough. Lock off all exits and move in with caution.
Ah, the sound of sirens. Did anybody invite the cops? NO! Are we going to let them spoil our right to congregate? NO!
STOP THE COPS! STOP THE COPS! ZOMBIES FIGHT AND STOP THE COPS!
Heard enough?
More than enough. Everybody to the exits. Stop the cops and zombies from clashing before somebody gets hurt.
Where are you going?
I'm going to see a man about a spell.
Shame on you, Val Rhymin! What you have done to these people is a crime!
What the hell...?
Mother of Magic! The Staff of One!

COCOON!
And YOU! Keep your hands where I can see them!
Get her! She's just a girl, you idiots. Get her!
AAARRGH!
Just a girl. Famous last words. Say hello to a girl of prey.
KREEEEEE!
Now... as I was saying...
It's YOU! You're the one!
The one?
You're the Minoru girl!

What? How do you know...?
Don't you know who I am? I'm *Mother!* Your parents and I...oh, we go way back.
You knew my parents?
Sure! We *"worked"* together many times!
Wow, it's good to see you. Nico! It's Nico, right? We thought you were dead!
Who's we?
The C.W.C.
Who?
The California Witchcraft Community...L.A. Chapter. Monk Theppie, Treasurer, at your service.
AAAIGH!
HISSSSS!
I'll take that, thank you very much. The *Staff Of One* is far too powerful for a child.

At last...The sacred Staff Of One is *mine!* All the power of the past, present and future at my beck and call! I am unstoppable! I am....
WWIIGHHHHHH!
AAIGH!
HELP! HELLP! AIIIIGH!
KREAUURRRRGH!
KREAUURRRRGH!
WHISSSSH!
KLUINK! KINK!

Nico, are you okay?
I think so.
I saw a giant eagle herding four goons to the police. I assume that was yours.
Yeah.
Are you sure you're okay?
Karolina... listen to me...very carefully.
Never... pick up the Staff of One. Okay? Never.
Things have changed.
Nico, we've all touched it before. Remember Chase...
The song... backwards?
Chase found the KZIT truck. Molly suggested the way to reverse the spell was to reverse the song.
Scary smart, that girl.
Yeah. Makes you want to reconsider the uniform thing, doesn't it?
Not really.

CLICK!
CLICK!
CLICK!
BEEP!
WHOOSH!
BEEP!
BEEP!
WHOOSH!
BEEP!
CLICK!
CLICK!
Aren't
ou going to
work?
Oh.
What work?
sniff They shut
the station
down.
Are
you going
to make us
pancakes?
No.

You girls did good yesterday.
Thanks. I wasn't scared once.
CLICK! CLICK! CLICK!
Me either.
BEEP! WHOOSH! BEEP! BEEP!
You girls are the future of super heroes. You know that?
Yep.
Mm-hmm.
CLICK! CLICK! CLICK!
BEEP! WHOOSH! BEEP! BEEP!
CLICK! CLICK! CLICK!
BEEP! WHOOSH! BEEP! BEEP!
THE END

10

LOS ANGELES. EIGHT YEARS AGO.
Dear Lord...
Anderson to command...
We've got a situation.
They're... they're all dead...
Sir, what the hell happened here?
Look at all this... this armor, this much firepower...these guys could have taken over Los Angeles.
Are...are these super-villains?
I've got a live one over here!!
Geez... look at the poor bastard. Whatever happened...he saw it all.
Sir... what could have done this?

X-MEN HEADQUARTERS. GRAYMALKIN INDUSTRIES, THE MARIN HEADLANDS. NOW.
Hi. Can whoever is inside my head telling me to come to San Francisco please shut up now?
'Cuz it's giving me a *really* big headache.

Er...hello? Molly, right? Molly Hayes? I don't know if you remember, but I'm--
Tut-tut! The less communicating, the less chance for mis-communicating.
You'll be wanting to see Mister Summers and Miss Frost, young lady.

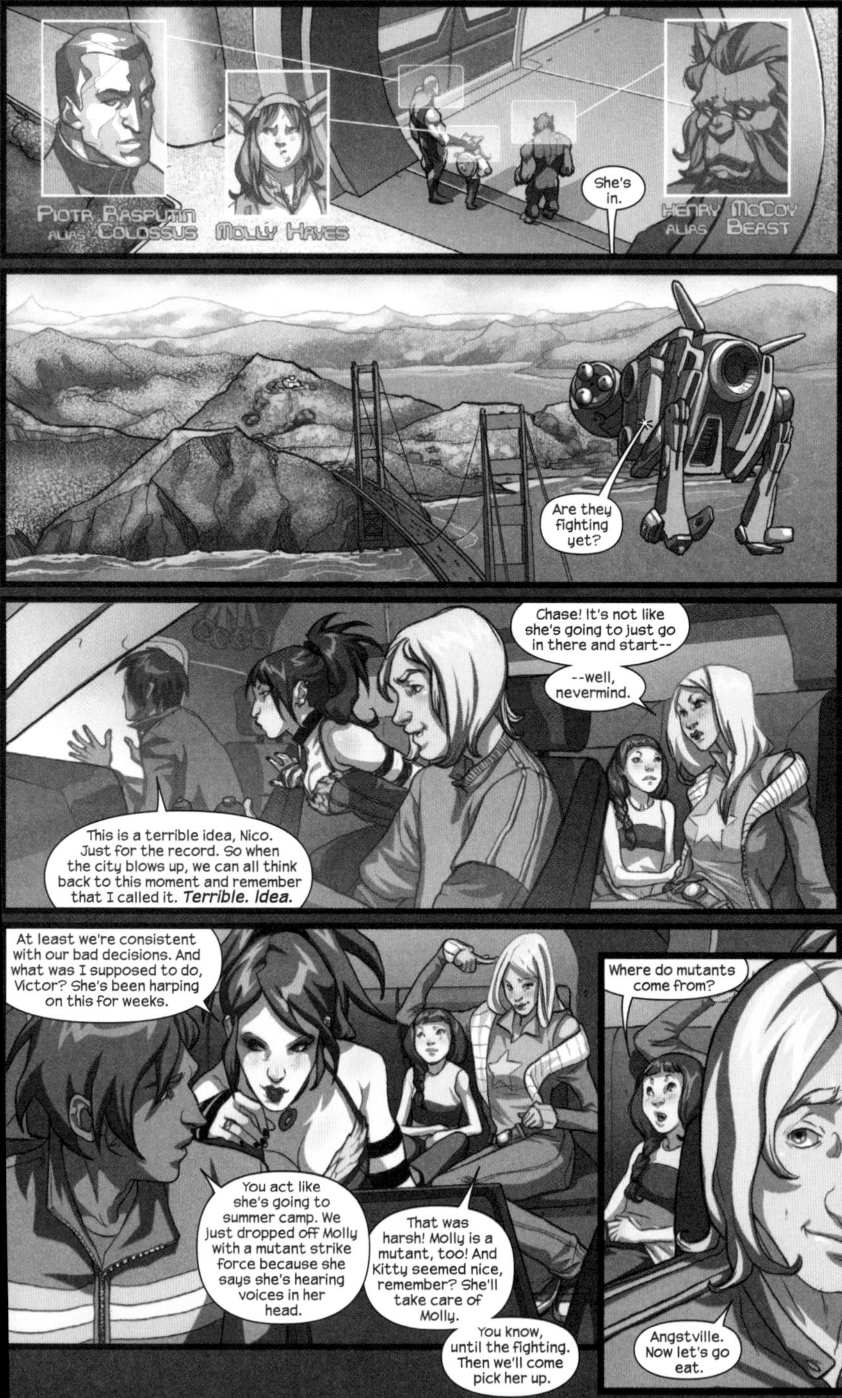
PIOTR RASPUTIN
ALIAS COLOSSUS
MOLLY HAYES
She's in.
HENRY McCOY
ALIAS BEAST
Are they fighting yet?
Chase! It's not like she's going to just go in there and start--
--well, nevermind.
This is a terrible idea, Nico. Just for the record. So when the city blows up, we can all think back to this moment and remember that I called it. *Terrible. Idea.*
At least we're consistent with our bad decisions. And what was I supposed to do, Victor? She's been harping on this for weeks.
You act like she's going to summer camp. We just dropped off Molly with a mutant strike force because she says she's hearing voices in her head.
That was harsh! Molly is a mutant, too! And Kitty seemed nice, remember? She'll take care of Molly.
You know, until the fighting. Then we'll come pick her up.
Where do mutants come from?
Angstville. Now let's go eat.

All I am saying is that we should have been more selective with our little invitation for all mutants to come to San Francisco.
I have very few limits, Scott, but being in the same room as...as that...it simply is not going to happen. But you...
...you're a bit afraid of her, aren't you?
What? No. No, no, no. NO!
It's just that... children don't like me. And you're much more... motherly.
I'm going to slap you. Where are the other urchins she runs with?
I sent a squad to keep an eye on them.
What are you not telling me?
I knew of her parents. The Hellfire Club reached out to the Hayeses, but it went...poorly.
They were monsters, Scott. The girl is better off without them. She needs a mentor...
...other than me.
Fine. I'm the leader of the X-Men. I'll handle this.
By delegating

WOLVERINE IS A JERK!!
I am going to kill you, Summers.
And he smells like beers!
I want to go with the tall shiny metal guy! Or the cat monkey guy!
What's he doing now?
He's... he's actually visualizing disembowling you. It's quite disturbing.
And she's asking for ice cream.

SAN FRANCISCO.
"This town blows."
It's *way* too clean here, and they've only got one In-n-Out Burger in the whole city. How do these people survive?
The lack of helicopters is kind of creeping me out.
I don't think you guys are being fair. We're in the most touristy part.
I wish Xavin were here.
Look, we're not staying. Molly's just checking in with the X-Men, and then we're gone.
What if she wants to stay?
That's not gonna happen. A) The X-Men are *tools*. They're gonna give her the tour, some sales pitch, and she's gonna hate it. And probably beat them all up.
And two, the X-Men are tools.
Uh, Chase... ixnay on the *"Men-Xay are ooltays."*

What the hell did that kid just say?
I think it was pig latin. Hang on. Ixnay on... what was the second part?
I think *"turn around"* was probably the gist of it.
Okay, see? This is why we should never leave the house.
Lord save us...more demons!!
Thaaaaat's not helping, Klara.
Whoa...if we're fighting, I get the silver girl and the tattoo girl.
Listen up, .A. chumps. We're the X-Men.
you're not.
Shut up! We almost are. And you punks...we're here to *"deal"* with you.
You wanna this, Fraggle Rock? Fine.
Can I grab gloves out of the car first?
Yeah, that's cool.

THE WORST TOUR EVER.
"So, there's a hallway. And over there is the bathroom..."
"Are you kidding me?! I wanna see the super hero stuff!!"
"...and there's the door."
THE BLACKBIRD.
Uh-huh. But does it talk to you? Because the Leapfrog talks to us, and it helps me and is nice.
And black is *boring*. But Nico likes black, and she takes care of us...so I guess it's okay...
THE WAR ROOM.
No, I cannot come home right now, Logan. This is my--who is that?
Princess Powerful! Are you really a Queen?! When I grow up, I guess I'll be Queen Powerful, but why are your eyes like that? Can you see okay? And your hair is white, how *old* are you?
I'm hanging up.
SCIENCE LABS.
If she doesn't shut up, I'm going to dissect her.
I am alarmingly okay with that.
CLASSROOMS.
Wait a minute...I'd have to go to school?!
Yep.
So where are all the X-Kids?
We keep 'em separated now. In case of rocket attacks.
...for real?!

CEREBRO.
Yes. If you happened to be in the bathroom when we psychically scanned for you, we *would* see you using the--
AUUGHHH!!
KITCHEN.
...and *then* we fought zombies!
DANGER ROOM.
Well, that's the dumbest name ever. What's the dangerous part? *Boredom?*
It's not turned on, genius.
I knew that!

What intensity level do you want it at?
Ten hundred thousand.
Level one it is.
Whoa!! What's *that*?
It's nano... nano-something. I don't know. It builds stuff for you to fight.
What kind of stuff?
Anything you--
A unicorn! And butterflies!
You got it.
YES!!
Okay, that is freaking *enough! Shut it down*, Prodigy!!
We're done here. I'm done.
HEY!! Turn it back on! I was still playing!
It's not a *game*, you little twerp! I don't know if you're keeping up with current events, but there used to be *millions* of mutants and now there's under 200.
We're not *"super heroes"* anymore, sweetheart, we're just here trying to *survive*. And maybe, if we're lucky, not go *extinct*.
So wait...you're saying you're *not*
You don't know what you're talking about. You're a spoiled little brat who lives in a *Fantasy Land*, and I don't have time to play mommy and daddy for you!

CRASH
So... how's it going with Molly?
You'd better pray that she eaves, because if she doesn't, I'm going to BEEP *kill* her, and then I'm gonna find you and BEEEEP BEEP BEEP you, and then I'm gonna BEEP BEEP BEEEEEP, right in the BEEEP head.
That's how it's going, BEEEEP
Molly, please wait...
Yes, please... don't walk away. We can call a taxi for you.
No! I never should have come! He's *horrible*, and you're all *horrible*, and you're not even real super heroes, and you're no *fun* and he was being *mean* and I just want to find my friends and *go!*
Molly, please give it another try. You wouldn't have to *run* any more.
All mutants are welcome here, and your friends would be too. I've already sent a team to check in with them.
You did *WHAT?!*
Don't you know anything?! They're just gonna *fight!*
Someone has to take me to them *RIGHT NOW!*

SAN FRANCISCO, 98 MILES PER HOUR.
So we have to make a stop... I'm gonna go get this special *sword*, and I need you to cut off my *head* with it.
SUTTER
No. And that's *gross*.
Your parents were all super-villains, is that it? You gotta be kidding me.
I mean, what the hell kind of super-villains raised *you*? Evil Care Bears? My Little Evil Pony?
Don't you talk about my mom and dad!
You woulda been better off if they made *you* evil, too. At least then you'd have a better picture of how the world actually works, 'cuz right now--
SNFF!
Are...are you smelling me?

BOOOM!!!
Hnnn!!! Kid...shrapnel... wound won't close... too much blood...
That's... that's gross...
Unit two to command...
We've got her.
You guys...are... toast...
My friends will... they'll save...

THE X SF DANCE CLUB ON HARRISON.
NO COVER FOR MUTANTS.

Hnnn... I'm awake, mom...I'm...
...hey. Are we back in the Danger Room?
3
Because this seems a lot more dangerous.
Just don't freak out, Hayes. I'll handle this.
This is your fault, isn't it?! Someone tried to blow me up because I was with you!
Man! Nobody likes you, do they?
You're wrong, Miss Hayes...we didn't come for him.
We came for you. It took me a year to find you, but now I'm finally going to have revenge on the Outcasts.
Your parents.

You knew my parents?!
Were you friends? I don't remember seeing you in any of our pictures, but maybe--
FRIENDS?!
Do you even know who your parents were, girl?
I...I know. They... they were super-villains.
Oh, no. They weren't super-villains, you little &$#@%. I'm a super-villain. What they were was far worse.
"My crew and I were going to make a play for a chunk of the Pride's territory.
"Your parents killed them all. Right in front of me. They did something to me...I had to watch. I couldn't stop watching.
"Whatever they did to me, I couldn't move...I couldn't talk...they had to put drops in my eyes to keep them moist because I couldn't shut them.
"I couldn't close my eyes to sleep. I almost went insane...but then it stopped."
After seven years, it stopped!
SEVEN YEARS!!

I...I don't believe you! My parents wouldn't do that...
Kid... kid, don't listen to this guy...
Oh, I'm not done, girl.
Your parents killed *anyone* who even *thought* about trespassing on the Pride's turf.
Your parents were cruel, sadistic *murderers*. They hurt people and they *liked* it...I *watched* them enjoy it.
They killed families. They killed *children*.
Anyone who stood in their way. Anyone who crossed them. Sometimes just for being *human*.
And now they're dead in Hell. So that's here I'm going to end you, so that hey *know* I got my payback.
Are you all done, tough guy? Or is there more to your sob story?
Because honestly? The girl here is more of a man than you are.

Kill him.
Close your eyes, Hayes.
But--
DO IT!!
BUDDABUDDABUDDABUDDA!!!
AAIIEEEE!!
EEEEEEEEEEEEE!!!
THUD!
Tell your parents when you see them.
Tell them that it was *me*.
SNIKT!!

RRRRRRRRAAAAAA!!
AAAAHHHH!!
BUDDA BUDDA BUDDA
SHUNK!
SHLIK!!
I TOLD YOU TO CLOSE YOUR EYES!
sorry!
BUDDA
AAIIEEE
SHRACK
BUDDA
GAAAAHH!

Uhnnn!!
THUNK!!
SNIKT!!
YOU WANNA TALK TO PEOPLE IN HELL? GET READY!
NO!
Super-villains kill. Not super heroes.
You're a super hero.
Not like my parents.
Kid...
I'm sorry your parents are dead, girl.
Sorry I couldn't kill them *myself*.

CHOOOM!
You okay, Hayes?
Molly?
My mommy and daddy were bad people.
They were always nice to me...they... they said they loved me, but--what he said...
No matter what that guy said... your parents loved you.
Because super-villain or not, anyone who could raise a kid as good as you couldn't have been all bad.

LATER.
"I want to go home now."
Mol...I know we were kind of down on the X-Men before, but you should really give them another try.
They're so nice! The students were so much fun, you're going to love it!
Seriously, Mol...you should--
THIS PLACE IS HORRIBLE AND YOU ARE TAKING ME HOME RIGHT NOW OR I WILL BEAT YOU ALL UP FOREVER!
Are you sure you don't want to--
JUST DRIVE!!
END

LOS ANGELES.
Hear me, Sons of the Serpent!! With this staff we will lay waste to our foes! Finally ours will be the power unrivaled! And we will be the salvation of these United States of America! Lo! These many years has this great nation been systematically poisoned by the inferior genetics of foreigners! Mutants! Space men! Robot people! And worst of all--
WHOOOOOOOOSH
Well, crap.

THE RUNAWAYS' MALIBU DREAM HOME!
So wait-- do these guys have anything to do with Cobra? As in "Commander"?
No. Totally different serpent commandos.
Mostly because these guys are real, and G.I. Joe is not. They're white supremacists.
So they dress up like snakes?? How does that make their point?
Are these guys complete morons or something?
They're white supremacists, Chase. So...yes.
WHOOOO-AM!
LOOK OUT!
Ahhahee ~sniff~ hee... ahh...
AGH!
Ta-daaa

Yeah, Karolina!!
Nice! No offense, but I wasn't sure you could pull it off.
Well I'm not surprised. You pretty much always amaze me.
Alright, K. That means it's your turn.
SNIFF! SNIFF!
Okay... Nico.
Truth or Dare?
I hate this.
Um, I guess--I guess I'll go with... man, I hate this game.
Truth.

Which one of us was the best kisser?
Okay, Nico. Since you're the one who would know--
Between Victor, Chase, me, and I suppose Alex ...
NO! NO FREAKIN' WAY!
DARE! I choose "dare"!
What?!
What was that noise? And why is everyone else awake? Can I be awake?
You can't do that!
It's too late, Nico! You can't tak it back!
Oh, Klara, we just got too excited playing a big-kids game.
I want to play!
No, you don't. Anyway the game just ended.
Like fun it did! You are not getting out of this one, Minoru!
That's right! To a big old creepy guy!
Yeah, when we met Klara she was already married!
So I'd say she's grown-up enough to know about your make-out preferences.
Besides, this is an easy one. Obviously I was the best kisser. Because Alex, our deviously departed leader, probably tasted evil--
--and Small Wonder here probably kisses all "01100011000010110010O..."

FINE! Karolina, okay?!
Karolina is a better kisser than any of you!
You kissed her, too? If I am to stay here, do I have to kiss girls?
You happy now?
Of course not!
I'm actually very happy now.
Great. Then it's your turn, Chase.
Truth or Dare?
C'mon. Do you have to ask?
Fine.
Then I dare you to stop acting like such a jerk, and for once--

OPEN UP!
Ngah!
C-C-CRAACK!
Ha! You missed! Too bad you only get one crack at each spell, huh, Nico?
Uh, guys? Is that... an egg?
Goodness! Your stick makes breakfast?!
Is anyone else wondering what comes out of that thing?
Knowing our luck, I'm not betting on *"omelets."*
But it looks like we're about to find--
WHAT THE--?!
CHOOM

KKKSSHH!
Oh, right. "Sons of the Serpent." I should have seen that coming.
How the heck did that thing even fit in the egg?
It's magic. How can the Staff of One be inside me, but I can still bend over?
Oooh. Good call.
I think about these things.
C-C-CRR
CHOOM!
Woah! Where did that one come from?
Split up!

Chase! Any idea how to take these guys out?
Clearly I don't. Fr the looks him?
Get some D&D c Try to rol natural 2
Guys? We got a problem!
Baby's having babies!
Nico! Klara! Look out!
Wow. Who's Quick Draw McGraw?
I don't know. Who is he?
If these things keep reproducing like this, we're gonna lose. Fast.

Hey! So far, they each had one, right? They don't, like, keep birthing?
Looks like it. But we'll never keep up--
Victor! Truth or Dare?!
Truth or dare?
Are you kidding me?
Fine! Dare!
Are you nuts?!
I dare you to eat the next egg!
Tough luck, Rusty. According to you, them's the rules!
Eggs up!
Fine! Fine! But if this thing pops out of me like Alien--

--I'm gonna mffmml nr fmmrmn!
BRRUUURZZZZZZZZZ!
Wheew!
Dude! How did you know that would work?
I didn't. But I figure you got a cast-iron stomach. And worst case scenario, we could always rebuild you.
Make you stronger! Faster!
You're lucky you guessed right! For a minute there we were all... worried...
...about me.

Ah, well-- I guess it's my turn.
Karolina, Truth or Dare?
Oh. We're still playing?
I guess, I'll go with "truth" this time.
You really only like girls? I mean, you never want be with a guy...
For the... perks?
e perks? Oh!
)h, no Not in the east.
And Victor, you ever want to e boys appealing to don't try to do it r I just got through estling creatures like that.
AAGH! WHY?! WHY WOULD YOU MAKE ME PICTURE THAT?!
Are you sure you want to delete selected memory?
You guys are such 'phobes.
I don't want to play with big kids anymore.
THE END.

9
VARIANT BY
DAVID LAFUENTE
RUNAWAYS

RUNAWAYS SKETCHES

BY EMMA RIOS

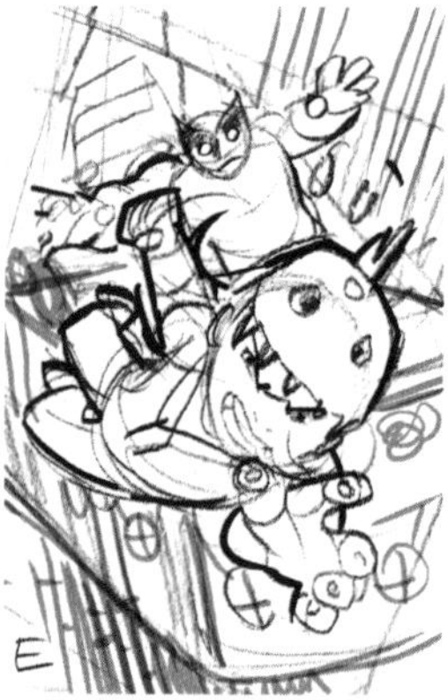

COVER #10 PROCESS

BY DAVID LAFUENTE

INKS

ALTERNATE COLORS